Andreas Weth, Roman Rochel

The implications of RFID on society. An ethical case study u
method for an ethical analysis

GRIN - Verlag für akademische Texte

Der GRIN Verlag mit Sitz in München hat sich seit der Gründung im Jahr 1998 auf die Veröffentlichung akademischer Texte spezialisiert.

Die Verlagswebseite www.grin.com ist für Studenten, Hochschullehrer und andere Akademiker die ideale Plattform, ihre Fachtexte, Studienarbeiten, Abschlussarbeiten oder Dissertationen einem breiten Publikum zu präsentieren.

Andreas Weth, Roman Rochel

The implications of RFID on society. An ethical case study using William May's seven-step method for an ethical analysis

GRIN Verlag

Bibliografische Information der Deutschen Nationalbibliothek: Die Deutsche Bibliothek verzeichnet diese Publikation in der Deutschen Nationalbibliografie; detaillierte bibliografische Daten sind im Internet über http://dnb.d-nb.de/ abrufbar.

1. Auflage 2004
Copyright © 2004 GRIN Verlag
http://www.grin.com/
Druck und Bindung: Books on Demand GmbH, Norderstedt Germany
ISBN 978-3-638-65311-4

Table of Contents

1. Introduction

This document contains a case study and an example evaluation of an ethical problem in the information technology environment.

In the **second chapter** of the paper the text of the case study is included. The Chief Information Officer (CIO) of a Mexican supermarket chain has to come to a decision about the implementation of Radio Frequency Identification Technology (RFID) in several stores and warehouses in Mexico. The introduction of RFID has major impacts on customers besides the possible selling of consumer data to a third party marketing research company.

The **third chapter** of the paper finally deals with an example case report in which William May's seven-step method is used for an analysis and a possible solution to the decision problem.

To sum up the case report, a conclusion is given in the **fourth chapter**. Lastly all necessary and additional information can be found in the **appendix**. Especially the attached research publication from MIT and Accenture "Auto ID in the box: The value of Auto-ID Technology in Retail Stores" should be considered for more detailed background information about RFID technology and its impacts. The publication can also downloaded from Accenture's website (www.accenture.com).

However as for most case studies, there is not a unique solution to the problem. Therefore learning outcomes of the case study are to not to develop the perfect solution the writers of the case had in mind but to see an ethical problem from different perspectives and to learn how to evaluate an ethical problem by applying a suitable concept for analyzing the situation.

2. Case Study

It is a lucrative offer, Alejandro Lopéz Martes, just received from Delincuencia Marketing Services (DMS). Ten million US Dollars in advance for selling customer sales data from all Mexican supermarkets during the next five years could solve some financial problems at Platano Supermercados S.A. de C.V. (S.A. stands for Sociedad Anónima and is the Mexican equivalent to a stock company whereas C.V. means that the company capital funds and stocks are variable) where Alejandro was working as the company's CIO. When this deal would turn out to be successful, it would mean a huge step forward towards his aim to become managing director of Platano Supermercados. The current CEO, Benicio Juaréz de Garibaldi would probably work just 2 more years until his retirement, but Benicio was already looking for a successor in the company, Alejandro knew. And Alejandro was on his list due to his success, his reputation and his strong academic background which is seen in Mexico as prerequisite for climbing up the corporate hierarchy. Graduated 15 years ago with a degree in Business Administration from the prestigious Mexican University Tec de Monterrey, Alejandro started at Wal-Mart in the early nineties but soon accepted an offer from Platano Supermercados in Mexico City and worked his way up to the general management.

It wasn't an easy time when he started at Platano Supermercados as the department manager for market research. Due to the high competition on the Mexican Retail Market and the competitive advantages of Wal-Mart, the most important player on the Mexican retail market, Platano Supermercados margin has continuously shrunk. Additionally the share price of Platano Supermercados has sunk during the last ten years whereas the share price from Wal-Mart was usually above average or on a record high.

But in spite of the harsh business conditions, Alejandro found colleagues he could trust and also spend spare time at the golf club.

One of his best friends and colleagues is Stuart, who emigrated from the United Kingdom to Mexico and is currently the Chief Financial Officer at Platano Supermercados. As Alejandro knew from his colleagues, he was widely accepted in the company for his business knowledge and his direct and passionate approach of solving problems. But for some people Alejandro seemed to be rude and offensive. Discussions therefore always occurred with the energetic head of the Human Resources Department, Cathrin Jontera de Vaqueros, due to her opinion that people should be better paid and treated with more respect at Platano Supermercados. Alejandro had argued with her countless evenings how to reduce costs without reducing the number of employees.

When he first read in a short article on the web site of Frontera Consulting, the consulting company which implemented the new enterprise resource planning software from SAP at Platano Supermercados last year, about the opportunities of RFID, he thought that it could be an opportunity to reduce costs and therefore increase profitability without firing employees.

Probably it would be a good idea to ask the consultants about a presentation and possible introduction strategies. Five minutes later he called one of the managing partners in the nearest office of Frontera Consulting and agreed on a presentation date next week. After the meeting with the consultants he was still sitting in his office late at night and thought about the most important sheets from the presentation.

The consultants also left him the research publication "Auto ID in the box: The value of Auto-ID Technology in Retail Stores" where the technology and the advantages of RFID were further described. He scanned through the publications and remembered the most important aspects. A faster and more efficient organization of receiving and stocking of incoming goods seems to be the major benefit for the retail industry. Physical

counting could be completely avoided. Theft of goods would be almost impossible. And there were many benefits for the customers, too. He remembered when he went birthday shopping with his son who was in a tantrum because the fan shirt he wanted was sold out due to the fact that one clerk simply forgot to order new ones. That wouldn't happen with RFID. Or the hours he had to wait in a row at Wal-Mart because there was just one check-out open. With RFID the check-out could be organized automatically and as fast as walking out of the building.

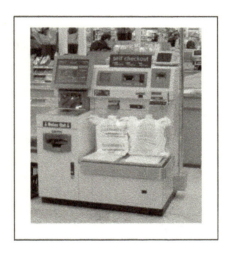

Alejandro glanced out of the window and watched the industrial zone where the head office of Platano Supermercados was located. Would the benefits be really as significant as it is stated in the research study the consultants gave him, he thought on the way to the coffee machine to get another cup of strong Mexican coffee? And implementing RFID would also mean to sell all customer data for the next five years to the marketing company DMS to finance the expensive implementation of the technology due to the insufficient cash situation. At a first glance DMS seems to be a reliable market research company based in the United States with international Fortune 500 clients and a simple but powerful business

concept of completing market research projects for its clients and developing strategies for the retail market. Alejandro met Joe, the CEO of DMS, a few weeks ago on a congress with the topic of the benefits of introducing RFID in the retail sector in Mexico. When he told Joe about his interest in RFID and the tremendous costs of implementing it, Joe made him instantly an offer a few days later to buy all customer data for the next five years if RFID would be installed at Platano Supermercados. Joe seems to be serious and trustworthy but he didn't want to tell what exactly he planned to do with the customer data because he was still in negotiations with companies interested in the data, he told Alejandro.

Alejandro thought about his wife and how she always argued against using his Lufthansa Miles & More Card because the benefits in her opinion don't outweigh the disadvantages resulting from privacy issues. However his wife also supported technologies making peoples lives easier like cell phones and credit cards which usually reveal too much of peoples private lives to some companies. Alejandro also read on the web about massive customer outcries in Germany about the test of RFID tags. What would happen when customers would switch to competitors not installing RFID tags to stay on the safe side? But the competition from Wal-Mart was strong and margins were still shrinking. Something had to be done and perhaps would it be better to avoid firing employees and to install the technology to reduce costs and increase revenues. Wal-Mart was already forcing his suppliers to provide all supplied products with RFID tags, he heard on the golf course from one of his former colleagues still working at Wal-Mart. Has Platano Supermercados the same power of demanding ID tags from his suppliers on all the supplied products? RFID tags still seem to be very expensive.

Alejandro also thought about the opinions of his colleagues in the general management. Cathrin would definitely be against the introduction of RFID but Stuart would support him, no doubt. About the CEO he wasn't quite

sure. Although Alejandro knew that Benicio held Alejandro's work in high regard, Benicio sometimes seemed to be old fashioned and risk avoiding. He probably had to further discuss his idea of introducing RFID on the golf course with him.

It seemed to be a tough decision, Alejandro thought in his car on the way home back to his family. Introducing RFID and thus selling customer data seems to have major impacts on customers and on the fate of the company, its employees and its suppliers. He definitely should think about a deeper ethical analysis of the situation before making a decision. Besides the risk of his own career the privacy of many people was at stake and if something should go wrong, the legal system in Mexico was well known to give right to civilians and not to companies. Loosing a trial in Mexico could mean paying millions of Pesos and seriously damaging the reputation of the company.

3. Analysis

In the following part of this report the case study is decomposed using the **William May's seven-step method** (Manford, 2004). With a case of a high degree of complexity the chosen model seems to be detailed enough to analyse the facts, the underlying ethical issues and to guide the problem solver through different alternatives to come to a substantiated decision. Nevertheless, as with all the other models as well, the provided decision is just one possible outcome depending on personal opinions even though the model allows for a high degree of candour as it is based on different perspectives and alternatives that are compared against each another.

First, the given **facts** of the case study are presented. This gives a good overview of the problem itself, the ethical issues connected to it, its stakeholders and other information that is useful. With these facts the different **ethical issues** that arise in the course of event for the different

significant stakeholders can easily be identified and additionally major **underlying principles** can be recognized.

With the now structuralized information **alternative courses of action** can be introduced and compared against each other. With **support of the underlying principles** it may be possible to decide for one "right" decision as many of these principles can be prioritized in a certain order. However, this is not an easy task itself as the prioritization of principles are highly dependent on personal and cultural views thus bearing a big source of subjectivity. Nevertheless both the **short- and long-term consequences** as well as **positive and/or negative outcomes** have to be assessed in the next step. The last step, of course, is **making a final decision** based on the given analysis.

3.1 The facts

The major issues of the presented case study can be summarized in a few sentences:

Alejandro Lopéz Martes , the CIO of Platano Supermercados S.A. de C.V., is facing a tough decision about commissioning a project to introduce RFID technology in the supermarkets and the possible financial backup of this project by selling the customer sales data to DMS, a US based marketing company. The RFID Technology has major advantages for the customers but with the selling of sensible customer data is also highly risky. This technology also supports the automation process that usually makes employees redundant in the long term.

This is just the dilemma Alejandro is facing from a business perspective. From a vocational perspective he also has to prove his reputation as a reliable and caring employee who is suitable to take over his superior's position as the next CEO of Platano Supermercados.

Personally he is expected to come to a conclusion which is in line with his wife's opinion on privacy issues.

Stakeholders:

To start with the analysis the stakeholder of the presented case need to be identified:

Alejandro Lopéz Martes:

He is the protagonist who has to make a final decision in the given case. Alejandro faces most other stakeholders of his decision and therefore has a strong need for a decision which is favourable for them but also for him. As he is in more or less complete control over the situation, this analysis can be assumed to be carried out by Alejandro himself.

Platano Supermercados:

Platano Supermercados is in enormous pressure due to the fact that Wal-Mart is introducing RFID in the upcoming months. Sales are not going well and the financial situation is also rather depressing. These circumstances call for a change in their business strategy to regain competitive advantages in order to succeed.

Delincuencia Marketing Services:

Delincuencia Marketing Services is interested in the customers' sales data of Platano Supermercados to analyse the impact of RFID technology at the point of sale and on the customers to be able to provide its customers with advanced marketing techniques and campaigns possible with the new technology.

Benicio Juaréz de Garibaldi:

Benicio Juaréz de Garibaldi, the CEO of Platano Supermercados worked many years for the company and was mostly successful during unpleasant business times. However, Benicio is looking forward to retirement and probably does not want to start huge new projects which could risk the company's continuity. Nevertheless he knows about the situation and that if nothing is changed the company will just vanish or possibly bought by Wal-Mart for a real bargain price.

Stuart:

Stuart is a very close friend of Alejandro and as the CFO of Platano Supermercados he knows about the financial situation and the outlook both with and without carrying out the RFID project and also with and without the selling of the customer data to DMS.

Cathrin Jontera de Vaqueros:

Cathrin, the Head of the HR department can be seen as Alejandro's antagonist as she is in fear that too many employees will be made redundant when the RFID technology takes off. She probably also is against the project in terms of privacy issues of both customers and employees as their purchases and work becomes completely transparent to the company and potentially to DMS and their clients as well.

Managing partners and consultants of Frontera Consulting:

The consulting company probably wants to push its clients to new technology projects in order to consult them in technical as well as in methodological ways. Their research reports and presentations can not really be seen as independent and objective but are created to serve their own business need. So this source of information has to be seen rather critical.

Alejandro's wife:

As mentioned in the case study, Alejandro's wife is strongly against anything that can be used to invade her privacy and that of her family. But she also sees the ease of use for the customers and for example finds that the positive aspects of cellular phones outweigh the privacy issues involved with them. Nevertheless she would strongly argue against selling customer data to other companies.

Shareholder of Platanos Supermercados:

The shareholders of Platanos Supermercados want to hear success stories because the stock price was not just outperformed by the index but actually sank during the last 12 months.

Employees of Platano Supermercados:

The employees of Platano Supermercados are in a tough situation. They know that either way in the long term some of them have to be made redundant unless the RFID project lays the foundation for an exceptional growth rate.

Customers of Platano Supermercados:

The customers of Platano Supermercados are not really satisfied with the service level at this stage. The sales are dropping and more of them are moving towards Wal-Mart as their supermarket of choice. Nevertheless they would probably return when the RFID possibilities lead to a hassle free checkout and products are not sold out due to an improved stock and supply management.

3.2 Ethical issues

Basically the decision, that has to be made whether to carry out the RFID project or not, brings about numerous highly ethical issues. If it will be carried out another decision has to be made about the funds for the project which then triggers even more ethical issues.

As already mentioned there are three perspectives Alejandro should consider in his situation:

1. Business Perspective:

Alejandro is the CIO of the company and therefore must be able to judge whether to introduce a new technology or stick with the old system. As an integer manager he also needs to be able to comprehend the scope of the RFID project for the company, its employees and most of all for its customers. The latter is especially important when coming to a decision about the selling of customer data.

2. Private perspective:

As a private person, Alejandro should run through a very thorough decision making process. This will help him focus on his important work and help him to justify whatever his decision may be. Also he should think how his family members would decide in his position to be able to understand them and make them understand his decision better.

3. Vocational perspective:

Because Benicio is already planning to retire from his position as the CEO of Platanos Supermercados, Alejandro needs to prove his capabilities. He also needs to come to a conclusion which helps him gain a better support from the employees because the management can only get as successful as the other employees let them.

These are the perspectives Alejandro should take into consideration. The given numbers do not indicate any priority because the importance of these perspectives is dependent only on the priorities of each individual. Nevertheless, the order indicates that from top to bottom more other individuals are influenced by the decision.

3.3 Major principles

As the list of the significant stakeholders shows, the impacts of the decision will affect them in different ways. These different ways indicate the different underlying major principles, values and rules that should be considered by Alejandro.

Integrity:

Emerging from the Latin adjective "integer" (whole, complete), Integrity means candour and perseverance in one's behaviour.
In this case study Alejandro's integrity is endangered by selling customer data for example.

Objectivity:

Objectivity means the ability to judge not by personal reasons but by generally accepted standards, rules and values. This implies that any objective judgement should not vary in its outcome depending on the person which is carrying it out.

Prevent harm, due care:

To prevent harm is a common goal and very close to the term due care which stipulates that a reasonable man should put a certain amount of care in a certain set of circumstances. In this context it means that Alejandro needs to care not only for himself or the company but also for its employees and customers to prevent them from being harmed by his decision.

Privacy:

Privacy is the ability to control the information about oneself and the degree of exposure to society or certain groups or individuals. In this case it is related to the selling of customer data to a marketing company based in a foreign country.

Business ethics:

The following ethical principles can be rather classified as business ethics in the provided case study.

Accountability:

This means taking the responsibility of one's action and everything connected with the outcome. It can easily be attained when acting integer because an integer acting person does generally not need to fear to be responsible.

Loyalty:

Loyalty means being loyal to somebody or in this case even to an artificial person, i.e. Platanos Supermercados. In the given context it means that Alejandro should act loyal to the different stakeholders of his decision and therefore he needs a prioritization to decide whether to be loyal to the customers, other employees, the company or even to his wife.

Obey the law:

Any business transaction Alejandro is carrying out needs to be legal. The law is a framework which should provide stable and secure ways to do business both for companies and customers. Here it is questionable if the law prohibits the selling of customer data.

3.4 Alternative courses of action

As already mentioned above the decision or decisions Alejandro has to make can be seen possibly two steps. The shown decision tree lists the possible alternatives:

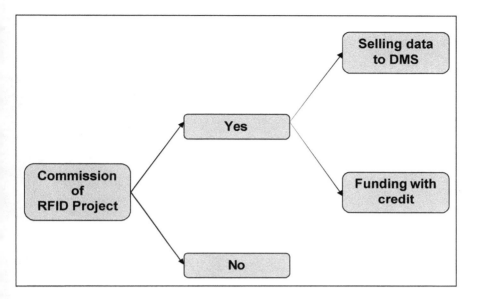

Either the RFID-Project will be commissioned or not. In the latter case there is obviously no following decision about the funding of the project. If the project will be carried out, however, the funding is another highly ethical decision with many stakeholders involved. With the financial situation and the stock price development two possible courses of action can be identified from this point:

1. Selling of the customer data to DMS
2. Raising a credit (Issuing a bond or more stocks does not really make sense as it would probably further burden the stock price development heavily)

3.5 Comparison of values and alternatives

With the different possible alternatives listed it is now possible to take a closer look on the values and principles that should be involved in the process of the decision making.

The decision over carrying out the RFID introduction or not is strongly connected to due care and to prevent harm which in this context seems to be a superior value as many important stakeholders are impacted directly and in a dramatic way. In the dreadful situation Platanos Supermercados is in, only a drastic change can prevent the company from going bankrupt in the long term and from the necessity to make many employees redundant. The introduction of RFID technology seems to be yet another step towards complete automation thus making employees redundant as well, but also can lead to the creation of new employments though growth and creation of new roles within the company. Concerning the given principle, Alejandro should decide for the introduction of RFID technology. But there remains a privacy issue as the RFID tags can store and transmit data that many people rather wish to keep for themselves. As the decision certainly is a business decision also business ethical matters arise. But they become more relevant when the new technology will be introduced such as what kind of data can be collected legally. Also Alejandro should be aware of keeping the necessary objectivity. He should not commission the project to promote himself to become the new CEO but to want the best possible outcome for the company and its stakeholders. Maybe it would be helpful to neglect the fact that Benicio will retire in the near future and to see if it changes his opinion towards the project. If this would be the case Alejandro would violate the principle of objectivity.

The next knot in the decision tree circles around the question of the funding of the project. Here it seems that all stated principles and major stakeholders are impacted. But even the due care principle can be interpreted two clashing ways: Due to the fact that the company is not in a very stable financial situation the customer data should be sold. However, due to the care that should be taken about the customers their data should never leave the company. At this stage of the decision maybe the law which is not really an ethical principle can give the answer. In

many countries it is illegal to collect and then sell data in such a way as DMS requests it. Consequently Alejandro should refrain from selling the data first of all because he should act loyal to the customers and secondly also because his decision needs to lead to legal business transactions. Additionally Alejandro should be aware of the connection of this decision to his integrity as well. If he decides for the unethical way, this decision will burden him in the future as he is accountable for it.

Accordingly, the ethical way would be to try to raise a credit. This way does not collide with the law but the privacy issues with the collection of customer data still remains. However, it will remain within the company and appropriate security measures can be completely controlled to ensure the customers and also the employees' privacy.

3.6 Assessment of the consequences

The consequences of the first decision will take a major effect on the further development of Platanos Supermercados. Either the company remains competitive and can regain customers and will grow; this obviously should be favored by the employees. Or the company will loose due to the high competition in the retail market and the employees will loose their jobs, the stakeholders might be compensated if the company gets taken over by another corporation but they too can face a total loss.

The second part of the decision could lead to a court trial when customer data would be sold. This would mean the company would have to compensate the customers and probably would also have to pay an administrative fine which would most likely lead to the end of Platanos Supermercados.

If the credit could be raised the financial burden for the interest payments would be negative for the company's cash flow. But in the long run this alternative could lead to a substantial growth for the company without troubling legal issues like the selling of data.

3.7 Finalizing a decision

Taking a decision under uncertainty with outcomes that can not be quantified is not an easy task. As it is already stated above in addition to ethical aspects also the financial background and environment of the company should be taken into account when a reasonable decision is made.

Focusing on the first branch of the decision tree - the question of commissioning the RFID project or not – it can be said that despite privacy issues the RFID project should be put into effect. As the Mexican retail industry does not seem to be very profitable due to high competition from Wal-Mart and therefore shrinking margins, Platano Supermercados has no other choice but to significantly reduce costs with RFID automation. Therefore privacy issues should be solved in informing all stakeholders about the benefits and other impacts of RFID and why the technology is implemented. In that way Alejandro behaves ethical - also from the view of his own private perspective - and all stakeholders are treated with respect and ethically correct, which is an important issue for analyzing the situation from the view of a business perspective. Concerning the implementation of RFID, external help should be careful analyzed as Frontera Consulting could not be the most suitable and competent partner for implementing RFID.

Concerning the next branch of the decision tree – how the implementation of RFID would be financed – the decision is also very clear when all the information given in the case study is considered. The offer from DMS sounds lucrative to Alejandro but the whole company is at risk due to the threat of a court trial which clearly violates the principle of due care and prevention of harm.

Also the fact that the CEO of DMS does not clearly reveal which companies would access the data from the research project sounds very suspicious, violates the principle of due care and would probably result in an abuse of customers trust in Platano Supermercados. In the worst case competitors would also get access to highly sensitive data from Platano

-18-

Supermercados and use that data e.g. for marketing campaigns trying to lure customers away from Platano Supermercados. Obviously the CEO of Platano Supermercados company wouldn't agree to such an option which is highly unethical as it violates several ethical principles, some were already mentioned above, like e.g. the principles of integrity, preventing harm, due care and obeying the law.

DMS´ offer sounds reasonable in the short term for an unethical solution to quickly access cash but as nothing is written in the case study that the company faces urgent liquidity problems, there is no need for a quick cash inflow which induces a very high risk of bankruptcy and is probably not legal.

Therefore the RFID implementation should be financed by raising a credit which could be backed up by assets to reduce interest payments. Issuing more shares or a bond is not recommended due to the underperforming share price. As no information is given in the case study about the exact company structure, the selling of assets or parts of the company for gaining capital is not taken into consideration and would be another ethical issue which should be discussed in a separate business case.

4. Conclusion

As RFID is probably one of the most important topics for many companies during the next five to ten years, many decision makers in SMEs and Fortune 500 companies will face a related decision problem. This shows why it is of great value to think about the presented solution and to develop an own approach how the decision problem can be solved. The **William May's seven-step method** applied during the case report can be used for almost any other ethical decision problem but other models offer different benefits and disadvantages. For a broader understanding of ethical problems, the reader is strongly encouraged to apply different models and discuss their outcomes. Concerning the proposed solution of the decision problem, until now no stakeholder except DMS has shown

unethical behaviour and this unethical behaviour resulted in a rejection of DMS' proposition. When the decision of realizing RFID and financing this project by raising a credit is proper implemented, almost certainly no issue of unethical behaviour will arise. As it is already stated in the introduction, this proposed solution is only the view of the authors from their perspectives. Probably a different model for the analysis, as it is mentioned above, will lead to another solution especially when cultural issues – how business is practically done in Mexico - are taken into account.

To sum up the whole case, it can be said that in the long term ethical behaviour offers in most cases a better profitability which is also a strong argument for most business environments where decisions are often made on a basis of profit or profitability.

Bibliography and further recommended reading

Cavanagh, Gerald F. (2004). Global business ethics: regulation, code, or self-restraint. In: *Business Ethics Quarterly*, October 2004, Vol. 14, Issue 4, pp. 625 – 643.

Heese, M. / Wohlers, G. / Breitner, M. H. (2004). Privacy protection against RFID spying: Challenges and countermeasures. In: *IWI Discussion Paper Series*, #11, July 5, 2004, pp. 1 – 6.

Kambil, Ajit (2002). RFID: Retail's 800-pound gorilla. In: *Logistics Today*, October 2003 Supplement, Vol. 44, Issue 10, pp. 34 – 37.

Manford, C. (2004). ISCG8021 IT in Society – Ethics and ethical decision making – Version 2. Unpublished manuscript.

Background information about RFID and the Mexican retail market

Wal-Mart attracts more RFID flak

Grass-roots consumer group Consumers Against Supermarket Privacy Invasion and Numbering (CASPIAN), which is fighting retail surveillance schemes, says that Wal-Mart's decision to tag individual items on its store floor using radio frequency identification or RFID violates a call for a moratorium issued last November by 40 privacy and civil liberties organisations.

Wal-Mart began item-level RFID tagging of consumer goods last week as part of a trial in Texas. Shoppers at seven Dallas-Fort Worth area Wal-Mart stores can walk into the consumer electronics department and find Hewlett-Packard products for sale with RFID tags attached.

Wal-Mart says that RFID tags in its stores are harmless since they contain nothing more than identification numbers. "While technically that's true, Wal-Mart fails to explain what it means for items to carry remote-readable unique ID numbers," says Katherine Albrecht, founder and director of CASPIAN. "It's like saying someone's social security number is 'only' a number, so sharing it with perfect strangers should be of no concern."

Albrecht explains that many major retailers routinely link shoppers' identity information from credit, ATM and "loyalty" cards with product bar code numbers to record individuals' purchases over time. The same will happen with RFID numbers on products, she claims. This means that if retailers can read an RFID tag on a product they previously sold, they can immediately identify the customer as he or she enters the store.

"Wal-Mart is blatantly ignoring the research and recommendations of dozens of privacy experts," says Albrecht. "When the world's largest retailer adopts a technology with chilling societal implications, and does so irresponsibly, we should all be deeply concerned."

The most publicised trial of item-level RFID tagging to date, Metro-AG's "Future Store" in Rheinberg, Germany, met with some public outcry earlier this year, culminating in a small protest outside the store. So far consumer revolt against RFID remains marginal.

(Source: Libbenga, Jan (2004), published online from the Register group www.theregister.co.uk, retrieved on the 22nd of October 2004 from http://www.theregister.co.uk/2004/05/12/wal_mart_rfid_flak/)

WAL-MART CONSOLIDATES PRICE STRATEGY

During May 2004, the total sales of Wal-Mart Mexico grew 4.5 percent, as compared to the sales reported in May 2003, reaching US$956 million. This is mostly attributed to the company's aggressive price strategy as well as its competitive advantages and to the economic reactivation. Wal-Mart also reported a 9 percent increase in total clients, for all different store formats. Wal-Mart is not a member of the national Association of Supermarkets and Departmental Stores (ANTAD) and yet, it is the strongest company in its sector. At the moment, Wal-Mart operates 322 supermarkets, 51 department stores and 271 restaurants. (Source: Agri-Food Trade Services, Market Information Latin America and Caribbean, Agri-Food News from Mexico Issue Nr. 16, July 2004)

WAL-MART MEXICO MIGHT BE INVESTIGATED FOR MONOPOLISTIC PRACTICES

The Mexican Congress requested to the Federal Commission of Competition to initiate an investigation about the supposed use of monopolistic practices by Wal-Mart Mexico. According to the Mexican Congress, Wal-Mart Mexico is selling products at cheaper prices than its competitors thanks to the vendor agreements that it has with its suppliers. Under the vendor agreements the suppliers are obliged to treat Wal-Mart better than to other clients and prohibit the suppliers to deal with Wal-Mart's competitors. The Mexican Congress indicated that these agreements have had a devastating effect on small and medium enterprises that cannot reach a similar power of negotiation. According to the Mexican Stock Exchange, during 2003 Wal-Mart sales in Mexico reached US$10.5 billion and reported a 65% market share in the Mexican retail sector (Source: Agri-Food Trade Services, Market Information Latin America and Caribbean, Agri-Food News from Mexico Issue Nr. 16, July 2004)

ANTAD PREPARES FOR ROBBERY CONTROL

Small scale robberies in supermarkets have been and continue to be a big threat; this is why members of the National Association Supermarkets and Departmental Stores (ANTAD) have agreed to invest US$87 million in prevention systems. In 2003, ANTAD members reported losses for US$36 million caused by small scale robbery of merchandise. Mr. Vicente Yáñez, president of ANTAD, stated that total sales of the association's members grew in 8.8 percent during the first 5 months of 2004. This growth trend is attributed to the overall economic reactivation and new supermarket openings. In total, ANTAD sales from January to May, 2004 accounted for US$10.5 billion. (Source: Agri-Food Trade Services, Market Information Latin America and Caribbean, Agri-Food News from Mexico Issue Nr. 16, July 2004)